The Real Story of Easter

Crafts by Christina Goodings

Photography by John Williams

Illustrated by Cathy Hughes

Contents

LION
CHILDREN'S

1 Who is Jesus?

Jesus is the Christmas baby.
Angels said he was God's own Son.
Shepherds came to find him.
Wise men from afar brought gifts.

Add stickers to complete this Christmas picture. What animals can you see in the scene? What sort of room is this?

Jesus grew up with Mary and Joseph in the little town of Nazareth.
He went to school and learned about his Jewish faith.
He learned to be a carpenter.
Then, as a man, he became a preacher. He chose disciples
to help him.

Can you count them?

2 About God's love

When Jesus preached, he told people about God's love.

"Make it your aim to live as God wants," he said. "Don't worry about money or the things it can buy.

"Look how God feeds the birds. Look how God clothes the flowers. You can be sure God will take care of you."

Add stickers to this picture.
How many birds can you count?
How many rabbits?
How many children?

3 Make birds and flowers

Flowers

You will need:
- paper in different colours and patterns
- scissors, pencil
- glue
- hole punch or round stickers
- extra decorations

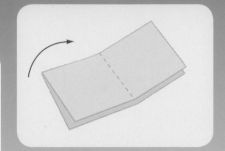

1 Take a square of paper 10cm x 10cm for the outer petal piece. Fold in half and half again as shown.

2 Now fold one more time, on the diagonal. Draw a curve to mark the petal edge. Cut through all layers. Unfold.

3 Choose different paper for the inner petal piece. Fold as for the outer petal but keep it folded to cut extra notches into the folded sides as shown. Unfold.

4 Glue the inner petal piece onto the outer petal piece with just a dab of glue in the centre.

5 Cut a paper circle for the centre and glue that on, or use a sticker. Add extra decorations if you wish.

Birds

Use these birds and flowers for a wall display, or hang them on thread loops from an Easter tree.

1 Take a square of paper 10cm x 10cm and fold in half. Copy the bird shape from the back page onto the fold as shown. Cut out.

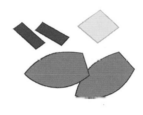

2 Choose contrasting paper to cut a beak, wings, and legs.

3 Cut or punch circles for eyes, and hearts and flowers for trims.

4 Open the bird piece up and glue the two legs, outer wing, and any head feather as shown.

5 Glue the piece shut. Then glue on the other wing, the beak, and the eyes. Add any other decorations.

4 Lost and found

All kinds of people came to listen to Jesus. He welcomed them all, good and bad.

"A good shepherd loves all his sheep," Jesus told his listeners.

"If a shepherd had 100 sheep, he would care if even one got lost.

"He would leave the others in safety and go and find the lost one.

"God is like that shepherd. God wants everyone in his kingdom of love."

Find the sticker of the lost sheep.

Spot the difference

Can you find 11 differences between these pictures?

5 Sheep and their shepherd

A good shepherd keeps his flock of sheep safe from harm.

Jesus said that his followers were his flock.

"I am the good shepherd.

"I know my sheep and they know me.

"I am willing to die for them."

See how to make the shepherd on page 11 and the tree on page 10.

Sheep

You will need:
- thin card in sheep colours
- cream paper
- scissors, pencil
- glue
- marker

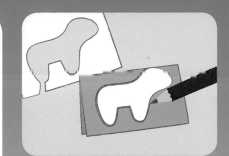

1 Copy the sheep shape from the back page and cut it out to use as a template. Lay it on a folded sheet of card with the top of the head on the join. Cut out.

2 Unfold the sheep shape and spread glue over the head section. Refold.

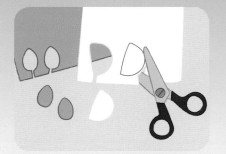

3 Copy the ear shape shown here and cut a pair in card. Copy the nose shape and cut a pair in cream paper.

4 Glue the nose pieces either side of the face, and the ears just behind. Add an eye with a marker.

6 God's good gifts

Jesus said that God was like a loving father, eager to give good things to his children.

"Any kind dad would give their child what they asked for," said Jesus. "If the child asked for an egg, what father would give a nasty stinging scorpion?

"God is like the best father ever.

"So when you pray, remember this: ask, and you will receive; seek, and you will find; knock, and the door will be opened to you."

Let this Easter basket of eggs be a reminder of God's kindness.

Page 1

Page 2

Page 4

Page 7

Bird stickers for fun

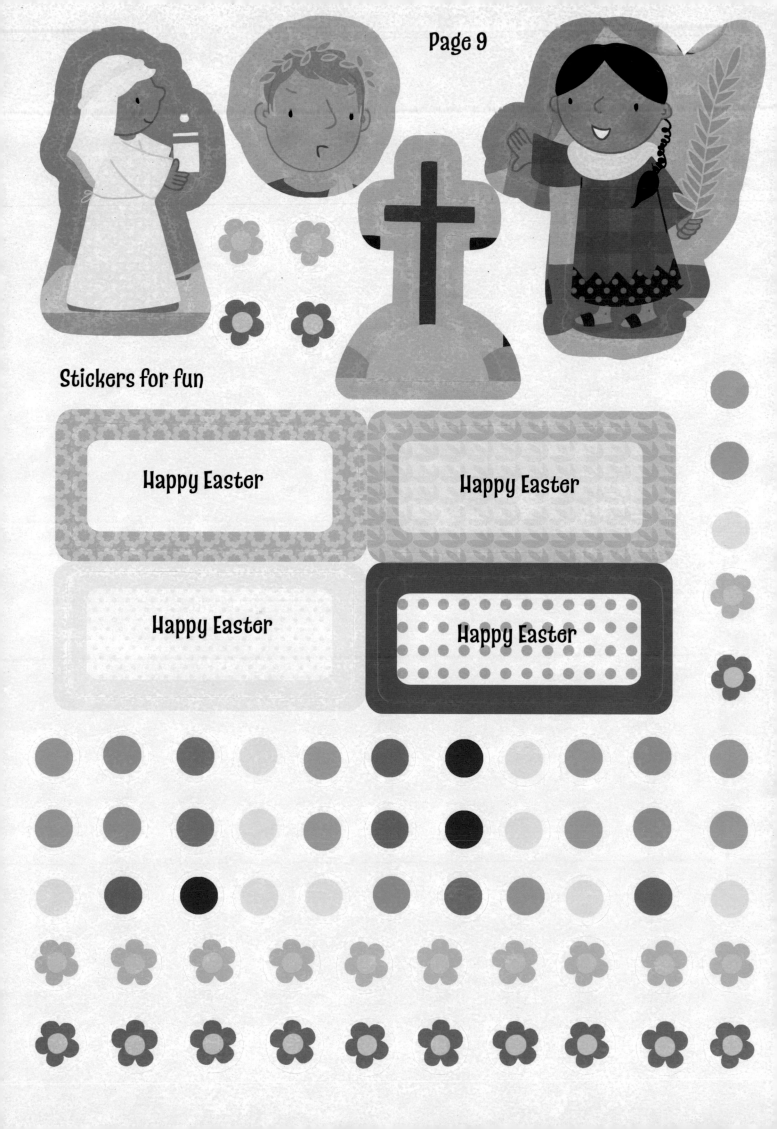

Stickers for fun

Happy Easter

Happy Easter

Happy Easter

Happy Easter

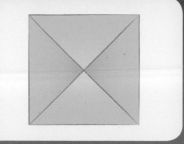 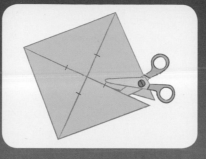 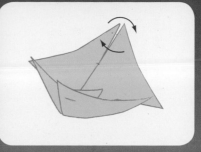

1 Cut a square of paper 20cm x 20cm. Fold diagonally, crease, and unfold. Then fold on the other diagonal, crease, and unfold.

2 Measure and mark a point on each crease 5cm away from the centre. Cut each crease from its corner to its marked point.

3 Take the two points of one corner and overlap as shown. Staple in place, or glue. Repeat for all four corners.

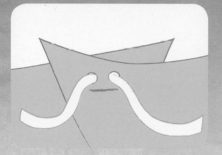 

4 Punch a pair of holes at each corner and thread a ribbon. Tie in a bow.

5 If you wish, cut a strip of paper for a handle. Glue in place as shown.

7 God's kingdom

Jesus said that to be friends with God, a person simply accepts God's love and forgiveness. Then they are part of God's kingdom.

"Children are welcome in the kingdom," said Jesus. "They even show grown-ups how to belong."

What toys and pets do these children have?
Find stickers for ones that are missing.

Jesus said that the kingdom of God is like a tiny seed that grows into a huge tree.

All kinds of birds come and make their nests in it.

Find pairs of matching birds in this picture.
Which one is alone?
Find its matching sticker.

8 A mother hen and chicks

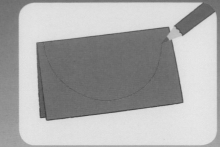

Many people loved Jesus and the things he said.

Others did not. Jesus already knew that the people in Jerusalem would turn against him.

"I would like just to put my arms around them, as a mother hen gathers her chicks under her wings," he said.

You will need:
- thin card for body, wings, and comb
- thin card or paper for beak and legs
- scissors, pencil
- glue
- sticky tape
- markers

1 Take a rectangle of thin card 25cm x 40cm and fold in half as shown. Draw a half oval for the hen's body. Cut out.

2 Fold another piece of card 10cm x 20cm. Copy the wing shape from the back page onto one side and cut to give two wings. Glue on.

3 Cut a piece for the comb. Make a narrow slit through the fold of the body piece, insert the comb, and tape in place. Add an eye with a marker.

4 Cut a piece for the beak and glue to the inside of the head below the comb. Cut a piece for the tail and tape to the inside of the other end.

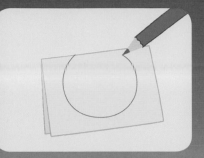

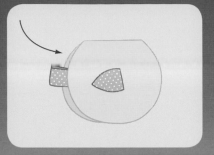

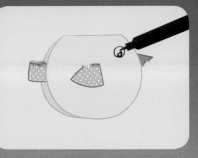

1 Take a rectangle of card 8cm x 16cm and fold in half. Draw an almost circle, leaving a bit of the fold intact. Cut out.

2 Fold a small piece of paper or card in half and draw wings and a tail. Cut out, then cut the wings along the fold and glue them either side of the body.

3 Use a marker to draw eyes. Cut a piece for the beak and tape in place.

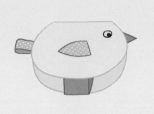

1 Cut a strip of card for the "legs". Mark into 3 and fold.

2 Glue the top of each "leg" and insert into the body.

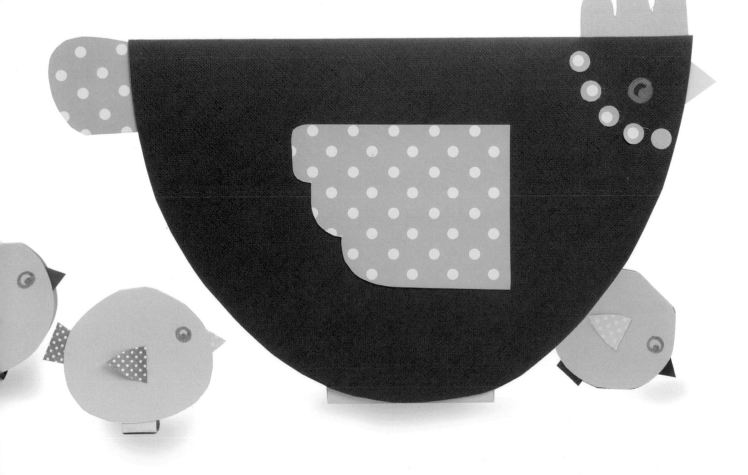

9 The Easter story

The time came for a festival. Jesus and his disciples went to Jerusalem. The crowds waved palm branches. "Hooray for God's king," they shouted.

Add stickers to complete the story.

One of the disciples, Judas Iscariot, was not loyal. He made a wicked plan with those who hated Jesus. He told them where they could come and arrest him.

Jesus was put on trial. People came and told lies. They said he had done bad things. "Crucify him," they said.

Jesus was put to death on a cross on a Friday.

His friends laid him in a tomb and rolled the stone door shut.

On the Sunday, some women came to say a last goodbye.

The tomb was open.

10 The Easter garden

Jesus' tomb was in a garden. On the Sunday morning, the women saw angels.

"Jesus is not here, he is risen," they said.

After that, Jesus' friends saw him alive.

The news of the Easter garden is that God's love is stronger than death.

You will need:
- thin card for trunk
- thin card for trees
- card or paper for stick-on shapes
- scissors, pencil, ruler
- glue
- flower paper punch

1 For the trunks, draw a circle with a 15cm radius (30cm diameter). Use a ruler to divide it into quarters and cut out.

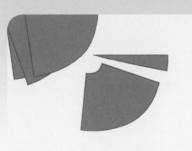

2 Take one quarter, trim away a sliver along one side, and cut the top into a curve as shown. Curl into a cone and tape, leaving the top open.

3 Copy the shapes from the back page to make branch pieces.

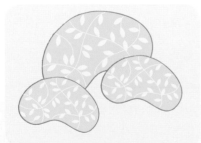

4 Copy the leaves shapes from the back page. Cut one large and two small for each tree.

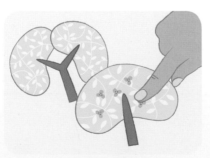

5 Glue to the branch pieces as shown. Cut or punch paper flowers to decorate the trees and glue on.

6 Insert the branches into the top of the trunk.

11 Easter people

John was a disciple. He was there at the cross, next to Jesus' mother, Mary.

"Be a son to her and take care of her," Jesus told him.

Mary from Magdala was a friend of Jesus. She went to the tomb to say a last goodbye.

An angel told her that Jesus was alive again. Then she saw Jesus.

Simon Peter was a disciple. Like the others, he had run away when Jesus was arrested. But he still loved Jesus and his message.

"Take care of my flock of followers after I have gone back to heaven," Jesus told him.

You will need:
- thin card for body piece
- paper in skin tones
- paper scraps
- scissors, pencil
- glue
- markers

1 Copy the body piece shape from the back page onto spare thin card. Cut out and use as a template to draw more body pieces on coloured card. Cut out.

2 On skin–tone paper draw a head the right size for the body piece (use the headdress shape in the picture as a guide). Draw the features and colour in the hair. Cut out.

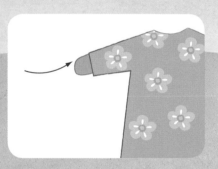

3 Glue the head on the body piece. Cut skin–tone hand shapes and glue these on the back of the arms.

4 Use the headdress shape to cut a headdress if you wish and glue on the back of the head. Cut extra shapes for a cloak if you wish, and add trims.

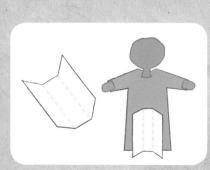

5 If you need to make your figure stand up, cut a shape like this in thin card, and glue on the back.

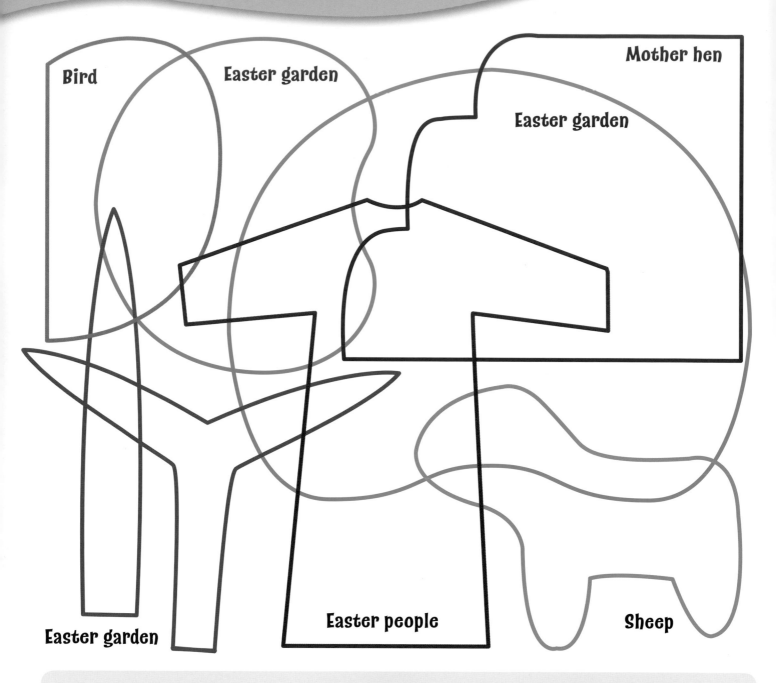

Bird

Easter garden

Mother hen

Easter garden

Easter garden

Easter people

Sheep

1: The room is a stable.
    There are 12 disciples.
2: There are 10 birds,
    7 rabbits, and 6 children.